SCIENCE AROUND US

Motion

By Darlene R. Stille

THE CHILD'S WORLD®
CHANHASSEN, MINNESOTA

Published in the United States of America by The Child's World®
PO Box 326, Chanhassen, MN 55317-0326
800-599-READ
www.childsworld.com

Content Adviser:
Mats Selen, PhD,
Professor of Physics,
University of Illinois,
Urbana, Illinois

Photo Credits: Cover: Thinkstock/Punchstock. Interior: Bettmann/Corbis: 7, 30-top, 30-bottom; Corbis: 6 (Adam Woolfitt), 8 (Craig Aurness), 10, 15 (Ariel Skelley), 18 (Franco Vogt), 20 (Carl & Ann Purcell), 21 (Neal Preston), 23, 25 (O'Brien Productions), 27 (Rick Gayle); Getty Images: 11 (Taxi/Jochem D. Wijnands), 13 (Digital Vision), 28 (Elsa); Getty Images/Hulton|Archive: 5, 30-middle; Getty Images/The Image Bank: 17 (Dennis O'Clair), 22 (Brooklyn Productions); Photo Researchers/Science Photo Library: 24, 26; PictureQuest: 4 (Corbis), 9 (Cesar Vera/ Photis), 14 (IT Stock Int'l/eStock Photo); Science VU/NASA/Visuals Unlimited: 16.

The Child's World®: Mary Berendes, Publishing Director

Editorial Directions, Inc.: E. Russell Primm, Editorial Director; Pam Rosenberg, Line Editor; Katie Marsico, Assistant Editor; Matt Messbarger, Editorial Assistant; Susan Hindman, Copy Editor; Susan Ashley, Proofreader; Peter Garnham, Olivia Nellums, and Katherine Trickle, Fact Checkers; Tim Griffin/IndexServ, Indexer; Cian Laughlin O'Day, Photo Researcher; Linda S. Koutris, Photo Selector

The Design Lab: Kathleen Petelinsek, Design, Kari Thornborough, Page Production

Library of Congress Cataloging-in-Publication Data
Stille, Darlene R.
  Motion / by Darlene R. Stille.
     v. cm. — (Science around us)
Includes bibliographical references and index.
Contents: Discovering motion—How things move—Getting going—Slowing down—
Motion in space—Relative motion.
  ISBN 1-59296-224-6 (lib. bdg. : alk. paper) 1. Motion—Juvenile literature. [1.
Motion.] I. Title. II. Science around us (Child's World (Firm))
  QC133.5.S74 2005
  531'.11—dc22   2003027228

TABLE OF CONTENTS

CHAPTER ONE

DISCOVERING MOTION

You discovered motion when you were just a baby. Babies love to watch things that move. They love to watch mobiles twirl around above their cribs.

You make things move all the time. You throw a ball with your arm. You kick a ball with your foot. The ball goes from one

A soccer ball is almost constantly in motion during a soccer game.

place to another. Anything that goes from one place to another is said to be in motion.

In the 1600s, a man named Sir Isaac Newton watched how things move. He thought hard about what motion is. He came up with three great ideas about motion. His ideas were so

Isaac Newton was an English scientist and mathematician who studied motion.

great that people named them Newton's Laws of Motion. Most of what we know about how things move, how things start moving, and how things slow down comes from Newton's laws.

SIR ISAAC NEWTON (1642–1727)

When Isaac Newton was a young boy, no one thought he was especially smart. Isaac was born in 1642 and grew up on a farm in England. He preferred making small windmills and other mechanical models to doing his schoolwork. He even quit school when he was 14 years old. His father had died, and he wanted to help his mother run the family farm.

Young Isaac spent a lot of time reading on his own. Finally, he went back to school and then on to Cambridge University. Even in college he did not act like a genius.

Then there was an outbreak of a terrible disease called the plague at Cambridge. The plague killed many people. Isaac went back to the country in 1665 to escape the plague. He stayed at home for 18 months. It was during this time that he came up with his ideas about **gravity** and motion. He also made impor-

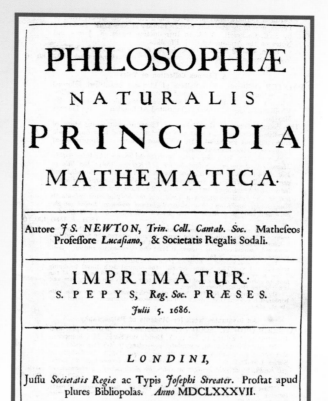

PHILOSOPHIÆ
NATURALIS
PRINCIPIA
MATHEMATICA·

Autore JS. NEWTON, Trin. Coll. Cantab. Soc. Matheseos
Professore Lucasiano, & Societatis Regalis Sodali.

IMPRIMATUR·
S. PEPYS, Reg. Soc. PRÆSES.
Julii 5. 1686.

LONDINI,

Jussu Societatis Regiæ ac Typis Josephi Streater. Prostat apud
plures Bibliopolas. Anno MDCLXXXVII.

tant discoveries about light and color, and he invented a type of mathematics called calculus.

Newton went back to Cambridge and became a professor of mathematics, but he did not tell anyone about his great discoveries. Twenty years later, some scientists found out about Newton's ideas and encouraged him to write a book. He did, and historians think *Mathematical Principles of Natural Philosophy* is one of the greatest books ever written about science. Newton became known as one of the greatest scientists who ever lived. In 1705, Queen Anne made him a knight in recognition of his scientific accomplishments. From then on, he was known as Sir Isaac Newton.

CHAPTER TWO

HOW THINGS MOVE

Things can move in lots of ways. Things can move in straight lines. If you throw a ball straight up in the air, it will come straight back down. The ball moves in a straight line.

A car going down a straight, flat road also moves in a straight line.

Things can move in curved lines, too. Throw a ball up and away from you. The ball curves upward and then curves back down. The ball moves in a curved line. A car going down a road with lots of bends and turns

Cars traveling down this road will move in a straight line.

Have you ever taken a ride on a merry-go-round? Merry-go-rounds move in curved lines.

travels in curved lines. A car traveling on a road that runs up and

down over lots of hills also travels in curved lines.

Things can move in circles. The horses on a merry-go-round

move in a circle. The horses go around and around as the merry-go-

round turns. Circles are made of curved lines.

*Many clocks use the back and forth motion
of pendulums to make them work.*

Things can move back and forth. Did you ever see a grand-

father clock? This type of clock has a long rod with a heavy disk at

the end. The rod and disk are called a **pendulum.** The pendu-

lum swings back and forth, back and forth, as the clock keeps time.

CHAPTER THREE

GETTING GOING

Motion is happening everywhere and all the time. Cars, trucks, and buses roll down the street. Trains chug along railroad tracks. Leaves and tree branches wave back and forth. Birds fly through the air. You and your friends run and play. But things do not start moving unless something pushes or pulls them.

A ball will not move unless you throw it or kick it. A car will not move unless a grown-up presses on the gas pedal. Pressing on the gas pedal makes the car engine turn the car's wheels.

This train cannot move by itself. What do you think makes this train move along the tracks?

Balls, cars, trains, planes, and even you have something called **inertia.** Everything made of matter has inertia, and everything in the universe is made of matter. Sir Isaac Newton figured this out. He told about inertia in his First Law of Motion. Newton said that inertia makes a ball, a boat, or any kind of matter keep on doing whatever it is doing. Inertia makes anything that is standing still keep on standing still.

So how does anything ever get going? The answer is **force.** An outside force can overcome inertia. In his Second Law of Motion, Newton told how a force is needed to get anything to move.

You can see how this works when you ride your bicycle. Your foot pushing on the bicycle pedals creates the outside force that makes the pedals move. The pedals go around and

A bicycle will not start moving unless the rider pushes on the pedals with her feet.

around, which creates the force that turns the wheel and pushes the whole bike forward.

The bigger and heavier something is, the more force it needs to get going. You can use one foot to make a scooter move. It takes two or three grown-ups pushing hard to make a stalled car roll.

It takes a lot of force to get a car moving.

Force goes two ways. When you push on something, it pushes back at you. Suppose you push on a brick wall. It is hard to imagine the brick wall pushing back on you. But it does.

When someone gets in this rowboat and pushes on the dock, the dock will push back and the rowboat will begin to move.

Some things that push back are easier to understand. Pretend you are in a rowboat. The boat is at a dock. You push on the dock. The dock pushes back on you, and then you and the rowboat float away from the dock. So you had better have some oars in the boat before you push on the dock!

Newton's Third Law of Motion explains how this space shuttle can fly into space.

Newton explained why the dock pushes back in his Third Law of Motion. He said that for every action there is an equal and opposite reaction. Space rockets had not been invented when Newton was alive, but his third law explains how rockets fly up into space. Hot gas rushes out of the end of a rocket. The hot gas pushes against the rocket. The rocket pushes back and goes soaring up into the sky.

CHAPTER FOUR

SLOWING DOWN

Newton said that inertia makes some-thing keep on doing what it is doing. This means that a ball or a bike or a car that is moving will just keep on moving. Balls, bikes, and cars want to keep rolling forever. So what makes things slow down and stop? Often, the answer is **friction.**

Bowling pins have inertia. They will not move until a bowling ball hits them.

Sliding an empty box across a surface is easier than sliding a box filled with heavy books across a surface because as the weight of the box increases, so will the force of friction.

Friction is a kind of force. It tries to keep one object from sliding over another. Friction makes it hard for you to push a cardboard box across a floor. Friction keeps your bicycle wheels from slipping when you turn a corner.

Friction comes from one surface rubbing against another. Every surface has lots of tiny bumps. You can see why these bumps make it hard to push the cardboard box across the floor. The tiny bumps on the box get stuck against the tiny bumps on the floor. A rough floor has bigger bumps than a smooth floor. Also, the heavier the object, the harder it is to slide. It is very hard to slide a heavy box over a rough floor.

You could pour oil on the floor to make the floor slippery. You could put your box on a cart with wheels. Wheels roll instead of sliding and go easily over tiny bumps in the floor.

Friction sometimes causes problems, but not having friction would make life much more dangerous. Friction makes your shoes stick to floors and sidewalks. Did you ever slip and slide on ice? Smooth ice does not have a lot of bumps. Smooth ice does not have

Even though friction sometimes makes our work harder, the world would be a dangerous place without friction!

This Zamboni machine smooths out the ice to reduce the friction between the blades of ice-skaters' skates and the ice.

much friction. Without friction, you could not walk. Floors and sidewalks would be more slippery than an ice skating rink. Your feet would just slide every which way. You would probably not be able to stand up.

Friction makes the brakes on your bike and your family car work. Brakes make friction that slows and stops the turning wheels. Without friction from brakes, there would be millions of bike and car accidents every day.

SEATBELTS, INERTIA, AND YOU

Someone once said, "It's not the fall that hurts, it's the sudden stop at the end." That person was really talking about inertia. Inertia can be a matter of life or death. Inertia is why wearing a seatbelt in a car is so important.

Something in motion wants to stay in motion until a force stops it. When you are riding in a car, you and the car are in motion. An accident causes a force that suddenly changes the motion of the car. Scientists use dummies to study what happens to people in a car that crashes into a wall at 56 kilometers (35 miles) per hour.

The car hits the wall and comes to a sudden stop. Inertia makes the crash dummies in the car keep moving forward at the same speed until they hit the inside of the stopped car. Inside the dummies are instruments that act like bones, brains, and other organs. The dummies show that real people would have suffered broken bones and other serious injuries in this kind of crash. Real people might have died.

Seatbelts help protect people in a car crash. They keep a body from hitting the inside of the stopped car. Seatbelts make a force that slows the sudden stop. Seatbelts slow down speeding bones and organs inside a body. By acting against inertia, seatbelts can save lives.

CHAPTER FIVE

MOTION IN SPACE

Everything in space goes around and around. Earth spins around every 24 hours. Earth and all the other planets move around the Sun. The Sun is a star in the **Milky Way galaxy.** The Sun and other stars move around the center of the Milky Way.

Our solar system moves around the center of the Milky Way galaxy.

What is the force that keeps stars and planets moving around in orbits instead of in straight lines? Sir Isaac Newton said it was the force of gravity. He said that gravity is a force that pulls one body toward another. Gravity makes the ball you throw into the air fall back down. The Sun's gravity keeps Earth moving around the Sun. Without the Sun's gravity, Earth would just shoot off into space.

Earth's gravity holds on to the Moon in the same way. Gravity makes the Moon go around the Earth instead of passing by it in a straight line. Gravity is the force that holds together galaxies, stars, planets, and moons.

Gravity keeps the moon in orbit around Earth.

CHAPTER SIX

WHAT IS MOVING?

Do you really know what is moving? Pretend you are sitting quietly with your friends on a school bus. No one is walking around. You think all your friends are sitting still.

Another friend standing on a street corner sees your bus come along. He waves as you go by. Your friend on the street thinks that all of you inside the bus are moving fast while he is just standing still.

Now you are at home sitting in a chair. Your

If you are sitting still on a school bus, the person next to you might say you are not moving. But if someone is standing on the sidewalk and the bus drives by, that person would say you are moving.

An astronaut in outer space would see everything on Earth moving as the planet spins on its axis.

house is not moving. Are you really sitting still? An astronaut looking at you from space would think you are moving really fast. You are spinning with the Earth as it turns around and around. You are moving with the Earth as it goes around the Sun.

As you can see, there is a lot more to motion than throwing a ball or driving a car. Isn't it fun to think about motion?

MEASURING SPEED

Some things move fast. Some things move slowly. How fast or slowly something moves is called its speed. You can measure speed by finding out how far something moves in a certain amount of time.

The speedometer on a car tells how fast a car is going. It tells how far a car can go in one hour. A speedometer is a dial with numbers. A needle points to the numbers. What if the needle points to the number 60? This means that the car will go 60 miles (97 kilometers) in one hour. The speedometer tells you how far the car will travel in one hour if it continues to move at that speed.

GLOSSARY

force (FORSS) A force is an action that changes the movement or shape of an object.

friction (FRIK-shunn) Friction is the force between two objects that rub against each other.

gravity (GRAV-uh-tee) Gravity is a force that pulls one object to another.

inertia (in-UR-shuh) Inertia is a property of all objects that keeps them at rest or in motion until they are acted upon by an outside force.

Milky Way galaxy (MIL-kee WAY GAL-uk-see) The Milky Way galaxy is the large group of stars that includes Earth's Sun and all of the planets in our solar system.

pendulum (PEN-juh-luhm) A pendulum is a weight that swings back and forth.

A pitcher uses force to put a baseball in motion.

DID YOU KNOW?

▶ Wind is a force that makes a tree's branches and leaves sway. Wind is moving air.

▶ A car can speed up or slow down. Pushing on the gas pedal makes the car go faster. Going faster is called acceleration. Pressing on the brakes slows a car down. Slowing down is called deceleration.

▶ You will never see a ball rolling up a hill by itself. A ball can roll down a hill even if you do not touch it. Gravity pulls on the ball and gets it moving downhill. Earth's gravity is a force that only pulls downward.

▶ Anything that rubs against something else can cause friction. Air can cause friction. Friction from air slows moving cars, trucks, trains, and airplanes. Air friction can make heat. The heat from air friction makes the outside of spacecraft returning to Earth red-hot. Spacecraft need a special covering to protect them from burning up.

▶ Pretend you are going to drop a brick and a tennis ball from a rooftop. Pretend there is no air to make friction as the brick and the ball fall. Will the heavy brick or the lighter ball hit the ground first? They both will land at the same time.

▶ Things go faster and faster as they fall. The farther something falls, the faster it goes. Pretend you can drop a brick from the top of a skyscraper. Pretend you can drop the same kind of brick from the second floor of a house. The brick dropped from the skyscraper will be going faster by the time it hits the ground.

TIMELINE

1564   Galileo Galilei (top right) is born in Pisa, Italy.

1589   Galileo begins teaching mathematics at the
University of Pisa; he develops laws about the speed
of falling objects by dropping things from the top of
the Leaning Tower of Pisa.

1642   Galileo dies; Isaac Newton (left) is born in
Woolsthorpe, England.

1665   Newton discovers that gravity is responsible for the motion
of the moon and planets in their orbits.

1687   Newton publishes *Philosophiae Naturalis Principia Mathematica
(Mathematical Principles of Natural Philosophy),* a book that explains
his three laws of motion and is considered to be the beginning of
modern science.

1727   Newton dies.

1879   Albert Einstein (bottom right) is born in Ulm,
Germany; his theories of relativity will change the
way scientists understand motion.

1905   Einstein publishes the theory of special relativity.

1916   Einstein publishes the general theory of relativity.

1955   Einstein dies in Princeton, New Jersey.

HOW TO LEARN MORE ABOUT MOTION
At the Library

Gold-Dworkin, Heidi. *Learning about the Way Things Move.* New York: McGraw-Hill, 2000.

Pipe, Jim. *What Makes It Swing?* Brookfield, Conn.: Copper Beech Books, 2002.

Royston, Angela. *Forces and Motion.* Chicago: Heinemann Library, 2002.

Whitehouse, Patricia. *Rolling.* Chicago: Heinemann Library, May 2003.

On the Web

VISIT OUR HOME PAGE FOR LOTS OF LINKS ABOUT MOTION:
http://www.childsworld.com/links.html
Note to Parents, Teachers, and Librarians: We routinely verify our Web links to make sure they're safe, active sites—so encourage your readers to check them out!

Places to Visit or Contact

THE DETROIT SCIENCE CENTER
To tour the GM Motion Laboratory and view more than 30 exhibits related to motion
5020 John R Street
Detroit, MI 48202
313/577-8400

MIAMI MUSEUM OF SCIENCE
To visit the Newton's Notions exhibit
3280 South Miami Avenue
Miami, FL 33129
305/646-4200

INDEX

About the Author

Darlene R. Stille is a science writer. She has lived in Chicago, Illinois, all her life. When she was in high school, she fell in love with science. While attending the University of Illinois she discovered that she also loved writing. She was fortunate to find a career that allowed her to combine both her interests. Darlene Stille has written more than 60 books for young people.